The Connecticut Colony

Bob Italia
ABDO Publishing Company

visit us at
www.abdopub.com

Published by ABDO Publishing Company, 4940 Viking Drive, Edina, Minnesota 55435.
Copyright © 2001 by Abdo Consulting Group, Inc. International copyrights reserved in all
countries. No part of this book may be reproduced in any form without written permission from
the publisher.

Printed in the United States.

Cover Photo Credit: North Wind Picture Archives
Interior Photo Credits: North Wind Picture Archives (pages 7, 13, 15, 17, 19, 21, 25, 27, 29);
    Corbis (pages 9, 11); Library of Congress Prints and Photographs Division, Historic American
    Buildings Survey HABS,CONN, 2-FARM,9-4 (page 23)

Contributing Editors: Tamara L. Britton, Kate A. Furlong, and Christine Fournier
Book Design and Graphics: Neil Klinepier

Library of Congress Cataloging-in-Publication Data

Italia, Bob, 1955-
    The Connecticut Colony / Bob Italia.
        p. cm. -- (The colonies)
    Includes index.
    ISBN 1-57765-586-9
        1. Connecticut--History--Colonial period, ca. 1600-1775--Juvenile literature. [1.
    Connecticut--History--Colonial period, ca. 1600-1775.] I. Title. II. Series.

F97 .I85 2001
974.6'02--dc21

                                                                    2001022146

Contents

The Long River Place

Before the Europeans arrived, Native Americans lived in present-day Connecticut. They called their land *Quinnehtukqut*, which means "Beside the Long Tidal River."

The Dutch were the first Europeans to explore the Connecticut area. But the English were the first to establish permanent settlements there.

The Connecticut Colony governed itself. The colonists built their own houses, grew their own food, and made their own clothes.

At first, Connecticut's colonists and Native Americans lived happily together. But eventually, they began to fight over land. Many Native Americans died.

During the **American Revolution**, there were many battles in Connecticut. The colonists won the war in 1783. In 1788, Connecticut became the fifth state of the new nation.

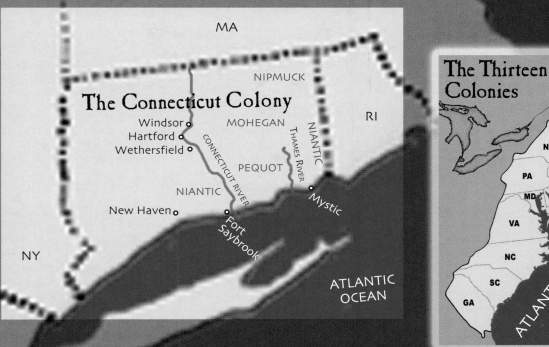

The Connecticut Colony

MA

NIPMUCK

MOHEGAN

RI

Windsor

Hartford

Wethersfield

NIANTIC

THAMES RIVER

CONNECTICUT RIVER

PEQUOT

NIANTIC

New Haven

Mystic

Fort Saybrook

NY

ATLANTIC OCEAN

The Thirteen Colonies

NH

NY

MA

RI

CT

PA

NJ

MD

DE

VA

NC

SC

GA

ATLANTIC OCEAN

Detail Area

Early History

Forests cover much of Connecticut's land. It has many rivers and lakes. Bays and natural harbors line its shores. Small islands lie off the Connecticut coast.

Before the Europeans arrived, more than 6,000 Native Americans lived in present-day Connecticut. They spoke the **Algonquian** (al-GON-kwee-an) language.

The Pequot (PEE-kwat) was the most powerful Native American tribe. Other Connecticut tribes included the Mohegan, the Niantic (ni-AN-tik), and the Nipmuck (NIHP-muck).

The Pequot lived in the south, near the Thames River, in **fortified** villages. They made clothing from buckskin. They grew corn, beans, squash, and tobacco. Hunting and fishing provided the remainder of their food.

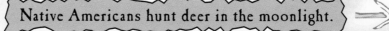
Native Americans hunt deer in the moonlight.

The First Explorers

Italian John Cabot was the first European explorer to come to North America. In 1498, he sailed along the coast. He was working for the English government. He was looking for a shorter trade route to Asia.

Giovanni da Verrazzano (gee-oh-VAH-nee dah ver-rah-ZAH-noh) sailed along the coast in 1524. He was also an Italian explorer. He was exploring the land for France.

In 1614, Dutch explorer Adriaen Block sailed up the Connecticut River. He claimed Connecticut's land for the Dutch. It became part of the Dutch colony of New Netherland.

In 1633, the Dutch built a small fort called the House of Hope near present-day Hartford. That same year, the English built a fort on the Connecticut River. It became the town of Windsor.

Giovanni da Verrazzano

9

Settlement

Though the Dutch made Connecticut's first settlement, it was not permanent. The first permanent settlers were from the Massachusetts Colony. Many colonists left Massachusetts because they wanted more political and religious freedom.

Their first settlement was at Windsor. In 1636, Windsor united with settlements at Hartford and Wethersfield. They formed the Connecticut Colony.

In 1638, a group of **Puritans** led by John Davenport and Theophilus Eaton founded the New Haven Colony. It was an independent colony. By 1643, many other towns had joined the New Haven Colony.

By 1660, the Connecticut Colony had grown quite large. In 1662, Governor John Winthrop, Jr., received a **charter** from King Charles II. The charter made the Connecticut Colony independent.

The **charter** gave the colony a strip of land 73 miles (117 km) wide that stretched from Narragansett Bay to the Pacific Ocean. This land included the New Haven Colony.

At first, New Haven Colony did not want to be part of the Connecticut Colony. But the two colonies united in 1665. The united English colonies took over the land. In 1674, the Dutch lost control of their settlements in the Connecticut area.

John Davenport

Government

Puritan minister Thomas Hooker founded Hartford. He believed in government based on the will of the people. So he and fellow Connecticut colonists John Haynes and Rodger Ludlow wrote the Fundamental Orders.

The Fundamental Orders was made up of 11 laws. This document provided for separation of church and state. It said all new taxes had to be approved by the people. Many people consider the Fundamental Orders to be America's first **constitution**.

Beginning in 1639, the Connecticut Colony's government was based on the Fundamental Orders. It created a General Court. The court met in April and September every year. At each April meeting, leaders elected six **magistrates** and a governor.

In 1687, Edmund Andros arrived in Hartford. Andros was the governor of the New England colonies. He wanted Connecticut to be a royal colony. He demanded

Connecticut's **charter**. But the colonists wanted the Connecticut Colony to remain independent.

The people hid their charter in a large oak tree. It became known as the Charter Oak. Andros never found the charter. Connecticut remained an independent colony until it became a state in 1788.

Thomas Hooker and a group of colonists found Hartford.

Life in the Colony

The early Connecticut colonists had to survive on their own. Men worked in the fields and forests. They also tended their livestock.

Most women spent their time caring for their families. They cooked meals and made clothing. Children helped their mothers by doing household chores.

People **bartered** with each other for the goods or services they needed. They bought other goods such as molasses, spices, glassware, and gunpowder from the few shops in town. They also bought goods from traveling salesmen called Yankee peddlers.

Religious holidays were important to the colonists. The English settlers celebrated May Day with outdoor parties and dancing around a maypole. On Easter, colonists held Easter egg hunts and more parties. On Christmas, colonists attended church, stuck holly on windowpanes, ate dinner, and went to parties.

A colonial woman cooks dinner for her family.

Making a Living

The early Connecticut Colony had a farming **economy**. Colonists produced food and products to meet their own needs. Families made their own clothing and tools. They **bartered** for goods that they couldn't make themselves.

By the late 1600s, the colony began exporting wheat and corn. Manufacturing started in Connecticut during the early 1700s. Clockmaking, shipbuilding, and silversmithing were the first important industries.

Some Africans and Native Americans who lived in the Connecticut Colony were slaves. They worked on farms and in businesses. In 1784, Connecticut passed laws against slavery. In 1848, slavery was outlawed.

In the 1740s, the brothers Edward and William Pattison made the first tinware in North America. The Pattison brothers became Connecticut's first Yankee peddlers. Yankee peddlers traveled in small carts. They went from house to house and sold many different products.

By the late 1770s, most towns had blacksmiths, doctors, weavers, shoemakers, farmers, cabinetmakers, millers, and merchants.

Colonists buy goods from a Yankee peddler's wagon.

Food

Most early Connecticut colonists grew corn. They also grew oats, rye, barley, peas, squash, turnips, and wheat. Some grew onions and tobacco. They also raised sheep, cows, and pigs.

The pigs were often slaughtered in early winter. The colonists cut the meat up into hams and bacon. They stuffed a meat mixture into the intestines to make sausages. They made lard from the pig's fat.

Connecticut's waterways also provided the colonists with food. The waters of Long Island Sound contained clams, herring, lobsters, and oysters. In the colony's inland waterways, shad were plentiful. Trout and other game fish swam in the lakes and streams.

The colonists had to preserve food to eat during the winter months. They salted and cured pork for storage. Beef was also salted or pickled. Colonists salted and dried fish on platforms called flakes.

A family harvests corn and pumpkins.

Clothing

In the Connecticut Colony, some people bought their clothes from England. But most colonists had to make their own clothing.

Men and boys grew flax on their farms. They also raised sheep for their wool. Women and girls spun the flax fibers and the sheeps' wool into thread. Then they wove the thread into cloth on a loom. They used this cloth to make clothes for their families.

Women wore dresses. Men wore **breeches**, tight-fitting jackets called doublets, and kneesocks.

Later, leather tanning industries began in Connecticut. Colonists made shoes, pouches, purses, and other goods from leather.

These men are wearing breeches, doublets, and kneesocks. $\Rightarrow$

21

Homes

Connecticut colonists built houses similar to those found in England. They used traditional English construction methods. The colonists used oak, pine, walnut, and cedar woods. They also used sand, gravel, stone, and clay.

Colonists built houses with wooden frames. They fastened the frame together with pins called treenails. Then they attached the frame to posts in the ground.

Colonists filled the frame with **wattle and daub**. Then they covered the house with boards for protection from the weather.

Colonists made roofs of thatch, bundles of rushes, and grass. But the roofs easily caught on fire from chimney sparks. So in 1627, a law forbade thatch roofs on new houses. This reduced loss from fire.

Inside the house was a large fireplace. Colonists made chimneys from wooden frames filled with wattle and daub. Usually, each house had one or two rooms and a loft.

Early houses had dirt floors. Later, colonists built houses with wooden floors.

Colonial houses had a few small windows. Shutters protected the colonists from animals and bad weather. Colonists covered their windows with oiled paper. Later, they used glass.

A colonial fireplace

Children

Many Connecticut families had five or six children. Parents needed their children to work in the house and on the farm. People without children paid their neighbors' children to help.

Men taught boys how to do farmwork. They cleared land, built fences, butchered animals, and split wood. They also planted and harvested crops.

Women taught girls to be wives and mothers. Girls helped with cooking and preserving food. They spun thread and made clothes. They also cleaned the house, washed clothes, and cared for younger children.

Some children went to school. In 1650, the Connecticut Colony passed a law requiring every town of more than 50 families to build an elementary school. Those with more than 100 families had to build a secondary school.

Some boys went to college to study law or religion. Others became shopkeepers. Some became **apprentices** who learned trades like blacksmithing, shoemaking, weaving, and printing.

Girls could not go to college. Most became wives and mothers. They worked on the farm and in the house. Some became midwives, servants, innkeepers, or teachers.

Two colonial boys help their father clear fields for plowing.

Native Americans

Relations between Native Americans and early Connecticut colonists were good. Colonists from New Netherland and the Plymouth Colony built trading posts along the Connecticut River. The colonists and Native Americans enjoyed a good trading relationship.

But later, the Pequot Native Americans saw the colonists as a threat to their lands. The tribe attacked colonial settlements. The colonists grew to fear the Pequot.

In 1637, Captain John Mason led a small army against the Pequot. Mohegan and Niantic Native Americans helped them. The army burned the Pequot fort at Mystic. Hundreds of Pequot died in the attack. This is called the Pequot War.

The Pequot who survived divided into small bands and fled. But they were pursued and captured or killed.

The colonists established two reservations for the remaining Pequot in 1666 and 1683. Today, Connecticut recognizes two Pequot tribes, the Mashantucket (mash-han-TUHK-it) and the Paucatuck (PAW-cuh-tuhk).

The destruction of the Pequot fort

The Road to Statehood

During the 1760s, England passed laws that set up taxes and hurt colonial trade. Some Connecticut colonists remained loyal to England. But most wanted independence.

The **American Revolution** began in the Massachusetts Colony in 1775. During the war, the English launched five major attacks on Connecticut soil. There were also many raids against the state.

Hundreds of Connecticut men joined the patriot forces. Jonathan Trumbull and Nathan Hale are among Connecticut's most famous patriots.

Connecticut Governor Jonathan Trumbull held office throughout the revolution. He was a close friend and adviser of General George Washington.

Nathan Hale was hanged by the English as a spy. His last words have become famous: "I only regret that I have but one life to lose for my country."

English soldiers prepare to execute Nathan Hale.

On July 4, 1776, the colonies adopted the **Declaration of Independence**. On July 9, 1778, the Connecticut Colony **ratified** the **Articles of Confederation**.

The colonies won the war in 1783 and created the United States of America. Connecticut ratified the U.S. **Constitution** on January 9, 1788. It became the fifth state.

Today, Connecticut is the third smallest state in America. But it is one of America's leading producers of helicopters, jet engines, and submarines.

TIMELINE

1498 - John Cabot explores the North American coast

1524 - Giovanni da Verrazzano explores the North American coast

1614 - Adriaen Block sails up the Connecticut River

1633 - Dutch build House of Hope; English build fort on the Connecticut River

1636 - Connecticut Colony formed

1637 - Pequot War

1638 - New Haven Colony formed

1639 - Connecticut governed under Fundamental Orders

1650 - Education law passes

1662 - King Charles II grants Connecticut Colony a charter

1665 - Connecticut and New Haven Colonies unite

1666 - Pequot reservation founded

1674 - English take control of Connecticut Colony

1683 - Pequot reservation founded

1687 - Edmund Andros tries to take Connecticut's charter; colonists hide it in Charter Oak

1700s - Manufacturing begins

1740s - Pattison brothers make first tinware, become the first Yankee peddlers

1775 - American Revolution begins; ends eight years later

1776 - Connecticut votes for independence from England

1784 - Laws pass against slavery

1788 - Connecticut becomes the fifth state

Glossary

Algonquian - a family of Native American languages spoken from Labrador, Canada, to the Carolinas, and westward to the Great Plains.

American Revolution - 1775-1783. A war between England and its colonies in America. The colonists won their independence and created the United States.

apprentice - a person who learns a trade from a skilled worker.

Articles of Confederation - the first constitution of the United States, written after the Declaration of Independence, and in effect until March 4, 1789, when the U.S. Constitution was ratified.

barter - to trade goods and services for other goods and services without using money.

breeches - tight-fitting, short pants.

charter - a written contract that states a colony's boundaries and form of government.

Constitution - the laws that govern the United States. Each state has a constitution, too.

Declaration of Independence - an essay written at the Second Continental Congress in 1776, announcing the separation of the American colonies from England.

economy - the way a colony uses its money, goods, and natural resources.

fortify - to protect a structure with a wall, fence, or ditch.

magistrate - a government official who has the power to enforce the law.

Puritan - a member of a group of people who thought the Church of England needed some changes, but wanted to stay in it.

ratify - to officially approve.

wattle and daub - a construction method. Wattle consisted of a framework of sticks and twigs. It was covered with daub, a mixture of sand and clay.

Web Sites

The Avalon Project
http://www.yale.edu/lawweb/avalon/order.htm
Read the Fundamental Orders at this site from Yale University.

Noah Webster House Museum of West Hartford History
http://www.ctstateu.edu/noahweb/
This site from Connecticut State University contains information on life in Connecticut in the 1770s.

These sites are subject to change. Go to your favorite search engine and type in Connecticut Colony for more sites.

Index